Stories from the Stabl

The Noisy Stable
and The Littlest Camel

Over the centuries, the Christmas stories
in the Bible have been passed on from
generation to generation. These delightful
retellings capture the joy, wonder and
celebration that surrounded the birth of
a very special baby, Jesus.

Bob Hartman is a widely acclaimed author
and storyteller. He is best known for *The Lion
Storyteller Bible* and other books in the *Storyteller*
series in which these tales were originally
published.

Stories from the Stable

Bob Hartman

Illustrations by Brett Hudson

LION
CHILDREN'S

Text copyright © 1998 and 2002 Bob Hartman
Illustrations copyright © 2004 Brett Hudson of GCI
This edition copyright © 2008 Lion Hudson

A Lion Children's Book
an imprint of
Lion Hudson plc
Wilkinson House, Jordan Hill Road,
Oxford OX2 8DR, England
www.lionhudson.com
ISBN 978 0 7459 6109 5

First edition 2008
10 9 8 7 6 5 4 3 2 1 0

This book has been printed on paper and board independently certified
as having been produced from sustainable forests.

Acknowledgments
These stories were first published in
The Lion Storyteller Bedtime Book and
The Lion Storyteller Book of Animal Tales

A catalogue record for this book is available
from the British Library

Typeset in 15/23 Baskerville MT Schlbk
Printed and bound in Wales
by Creative Print and Design

The Noisy Stable

Tales of the Nativity

The Littlest camel

christmas tales and legends from around the world

The Noisy Stable

Stable

Tales of the Nativity

Contents

All these retellings are based on stories in the first four books of the New Testament part of the Bible.

A Surprise for Zechariah

Gabriel was an angel. A very busy angel.

God decided that the time had come to send his Son into the world. So he chose Gabriel to get everything ready.

The first thing Gabriel did was to visit an old priest called Zechariah. He and his wife, Elizabeth, had no children of their own. And that made them very sad. So, one day, while Zechariah was working in the temple in

Jerusalem, Gabriel appeared to him – bright and shiny, glowing and gold!

Zechariah had never seen an angel before, so he was very frightened. His legs turned to jelly. He quivered, he shivered and he shook.

'Don't be afraid,' said Gabriel gently. 'For I am here to bring you good news! You and your wife have been praying for a child, and soon your prayers will be answered. You will have a baby. You will call him John. And when he grows up, he will help the world get ready to meet God's own special Son!'

'But my wife and I are so old. How can we possibly have a child?' said Zechariah.

'I'll prove it to you,' said Gabriel with a smile. 'From now until the time the child is born, you will not be able to speak a word. That way you will know what I say is true.'

Zechariah opened his mouth to answer the angel. But nothing came out. Not a word. Not a whisper. Not a sound!

So he staggered out of the temple – eyes wide open and lips shut tight. And it wasn't long before his wife came to him with the most amazing news.

'I'm going to have a baby!' she cried, tears of joy streaming down her face. 'After all these years, our prayers have been answered!'

Zechariah wanted to say, 'I know.' He wanted to say, 'The angel told me this would happen.' He wanted to shout 'Hooray!' But all he could do was smile. And that smile said more than enough!

A Surprise for Mary

That busy angel Gabriel went to work again.

Six months after Elizabeth discovered that she would have a child, he visited Elizabeth's cousin, Mary.

Mary and Elizabeth were quite different.

Elizabeth lived in the south, near the big city of Jerusalem. But Mary lived further north, in a little town called Nazareth.

Elizabeth was old. But Mary was young.

And Elizabeth had been married for many years, but Mary had never been married at all. She was engaged, however, to a carpenter named Joseph.

Mary was in her house, one day, dreaming of the wedding and the life that she and Joseph would share together. And that's when Gabriel appeared to her – bright and shiny, glowing and gold – just as he'd appeared to old Zechariah.

'Hello, Mary,' Gabriel said. 'God is with you and wants to do something very special for you.'

Mary didn't know what to think. She had never seen an angel before. And as for God wanting to do something special for her, well, she couldn't imagine what that might

be. She was too scared to ask, and Gabriel could see the worry in her eyes.

'There's no need to be afraid,' he told her. 'God has chosen you for something wonderful. He wants you to be the mother of a little baby, a baby called Jesus.'

Mary looked more worried than ever. And puzzled too.

'I don't understand,' she said. 'How can I have a baby when I don't yet have a husband?'

Gabriel smiled. It was a warm smile. And a mysterious smile too.

'God's own Spirit will visit you,' he said. 'Like a welcome shadow on a warm summer's day, he will cover you and wrap himself around you. And the child who will spring to life in you will be God's child too.'

Mary was shaking now. Her eyes were wide open, amazed. Her mouth dropped open too. She had never heard anything like this before!

'I know this is hard to believe,' Gabriel went on. 'But God can do the most amazing things. Why, your own cousin, Elizabeth – that's right, Elizabeth, who could never have

a child before – is expecting a baby too!
Impossible? Not for God! So what do you
say, Mary? Will you be the mother of God's
Son?'

Mary shut her eyes. She shut her mouth
too. She looked just as if she was praying.

What will Joseph think, she wondered,
when he hears about the child? He is bound
to think the worst. And my parents too.

Their plans, all their plans, will be ruined! And yet, God has a plan as well. And he has chosen me – me of all people – to be a part of that plan. What can I do but say yes?

And so Mary nodded. Eyes still shut, head bowed in prayer, she nodded.

'I will do it,' she said. 'I will be the mother of God's Son.'

And when she opened her eyes, the angel was gone.

Mary had to tell someone!

The news that the angel Gabriel had given her was so amazing that it seemed almost too good to be true. So Mary hurried to visit the one person in the world she thought would understand – her cousin, Elizabeth.

Elizabeth was expecting a child of her

own, remember? It was the son that Gabriel
(that busy angel!) had promised to her and
her husband, Zechariah.

Mary said 'Hello' to her cousin. But
instead of saying 'Hello' back, Elizabeth said
a surprised 'Ooh!'

'It's my baby!' she chuckled. 'When you
said, 'Hello' he jumped! He jumped for joy,

inside me! He knows – don't you see? – that the baby who is growing inside you is God's own Son.'

Elizabeth knew! She already knew! Even before Mary could tell her. Now Mary was more amazed than ever.

'God has done something wonderful for you,' said Elizabeth to Mary. 'And you have to trust that it will all come true – just as the angel told you.'

Mary nodded, 'I do. I really do.' And then she paused. And then she thought. And then she spoke again – as if she was making up a poem, or singing her own special song:

God has been so good to me
And I simply don't deserve it.
I'm nothing. A nobody.
Yet God has chosen me
To be the mother of his Son!

And one day – I'm sure of this –
Everyone will know my name
And be able to tell my story.
That's how God works, isn't it?
He knocks down the mighty and proud
And lifts up those who are small and weak.
He sends the rich away hungry.
And he feeds the hungry until they're full!
He has watched over his people, Israel,
From the time of our father, Abraham.
And now, praise God, he's watching over me!

When she had finished, Mary hugged her cousin, Elizabeth. Then she stayed with her for three months more, until Elizabeth's baby, John, was born, and then returned to her home in Nazareth.

A Name for the Baby

What will you call him? Tell us his name!'

That's what everyone wanted to know: Elizabeth's sisters and brothers. Her nieces and nephews. Her cousins and neighbours and friends.

They had all come round to celebrate the birth of her son. They knew how long she had prayed. They knew how long she had waited. They had shared her surprised delight when she discovered that she would be having a child at last. And now they wanted to know his name.

'Perhaps you will name him after dear Uncle Ezra,' suggested one of her sisters.

'Or Grandfather Saul,' suggested another. 'Look! He has his smile!'

'Or what about our father?' added one of her brothers. 'It would be such an honour!'

And that's when Elizabeth held up her hand. 'We have already decided on a name,' she announced. 'We will call him John.'

The room went quiet for a moment.

And then Elizabeth's oldest sister asked the question that everyone wanted to hear. 'But why do that? No one in our family has ever been called John.'

And that's when Elizabeth turned to her husband, Zechariah. He had been sitting there quietly (for that busy angel Gabriel had taken away his voice – remember?).

Zechariah nodded and smiled a mysterious smile. Then he picked up a writing tablet and wrote on it, clearly, so that everyone could see, 'His name is John.' And the minute he did so, Zechariah could speak again!

'Praise God!' he shouted. And he didn't stop talking until he had told them everything about the angel's visit and God's promise and how Gabriel had told him

exactly what the child's name would be.

'This boy will be something special!' he concluded. 'God has great plans for him.'

And so God did. For when little John grew

up, he went to live in the wilderness. He ate locusts for his supper and wild honey for his dessert. And he told God's people to change their ways and to be sorry for the wrong things that they had done, so that they would be ready to meet God's own special Son.

Joseph's Dream

Joseph the carpenter was not very happy.
Not very happy at all. The girl he had
planned to marry was going to have a baby,
but the baby was not his.

Mary had tried to explain. She had told
him about the angel and what the angel had
said. She had told him that the baby would
be God's special Son. But Joseph did not
believe her. And who could blame him? For

the story was so amazing that Mary hardly believed it herself!

In the end, Joseph decided to call off the wedding – quietly, of course, so that Mary would not be embarrassed. And that was when that busy angel, Gabriel, decided to make another visit.

He appeared to Joseph in a dream – bright and shiny, glowing and gold – deep in the middle of the night.

'There's no need to be worried,' he said to Joseph. 'There's no need to be afraid. Everything Mary has told you is true. The baby she is carrying is God's own special Son. When he is born, God wants you to call him Jesus. His name means "God saves". And when he grows up, that is exactly what he will do. He will be "God among us",

"God come to save us" from everything that is wicked and wrong.'

When Joseph woke up, he knew exactly what to do. He went straight to Mary's house. He hugged her and told her he was sorry that he had not believed her. Then, just as soon as he could, he married her. And he took her home to be his wife.

Time to Be Counted

Mary counted the months.

One, two, three.

Four, five, six.

Seven, eight and nine.

It was almost time for her baby to be born!

Mary counted the blankets. Mary counted the towels. And then Mary smiled. For everything was ready – ready for the birth of God's own special Son.

But somebody else was counting too. And all Mary's plans were about to be ruined.

'It's the Emperor!' sighed Joseph, as he walked into the house. 'He wants to count everyone in the country. Everyone! And to make it easy for him, we have to go back to my home town.'

'Your home town?' cried Mary. 'But that means we have to go all the way to…'

'… Bethlehem!' sighed Joseph again.

'A week's journey, at least! And you with the baby coming.'

'I can't do it,' wept Mary. And the tears rolled down her cheeks.

One, two, three.

Four, five, six.

Seven, eight and nine.

Joseph counted each tear. Then he wiped them all away.

'But you must,' he said gently. 'It's the law.'

Then he held her and kissed her and he added more gently still, 'God is with you. Remember? That's what the angel told you. And if God is with you, then he will help you to make this journey. It's his promise,' said Joseph with a smile. 'So you can count on it!'

A Long Journey

One, two, three.

Four, five, six.

Seven, eight and nine.

Mary counted the miles. And the donkey's footsteps. And the number of times the little baby kicked inside her belly.

It was a long trip. And a hot trip. And she prayed that it would soon be over.

One, two, three.

Four, five, six.

Seven, eight and nine.

Mary knew, because she counted, that there were many more miles to go.

When they arrived, at last, in Bethlehem, Mary and Joseph looked for a place to stay.

One, two, three.

Four, five, six.

Seven, eight and nine.

They knocked on door after door.

But at every door, the answer was the same. 'We have no room here! Go away!'

Mary began to cry.

'It's the baby!' she wept. 'The baby is coming. And I need somewhere to rest.'

So Joseph looked up and down the street once more.

One, two, three.

Four, five, six.

Seven, eight and nine.

And there, at house number ten, he found a door he had missed!

The door opened. The innkeeper smiled. But when Joseph asked if he had an empty room, the innkeeper sadly shook his head.

'Bethlehem is bursting,' he said with a sigh. 'We have no room at all.'

'But my wife…' Joseph pleaded. 'My wife is about to have a baby.'

'I can see that,' the innkeeper nodded. 'But I'm sorry, there's nothing I can do.' And he started to close the door.

'Please!' Joseph cried.

'Please!' wept Mary as well.

And that's when the door swung open again.

'There is a place,' nodded the innkeeper. 'Back behind the inn. It's nothing fancy,

mind you. But it's warm and clean and dry.
And you can have your baby safely there.'

So he led them to the stable. And there,
among the animals, Mary finally lay down
and gave birth to God's own special Son.

The Noisy Stable

It was nothing special. Just an ordinary stable. Filled with ordinary stable sounds.

The deep 'moo' of a big black cow.

The noisy 'hee-haw' of a little brown donkey.

The 'coo' of a dove, the 'baa' of a lamb, and the 'scrickety-scrack' of a spider, skittering along the wall.

But then there came another sound. An

out-of-the-ordinary sound. A sound that had never been heard in this stable before the sharp 'waa-waa!' of a newborn baby.

It was Mary's baby, of course. The baby the angel Gabriel had promised her. But there was nothing ordinary about him. For he was Jesus, God's own special Son.

The cow went 'moo'.

The donkey brayed 'hee-haw'.

The dove called 'coo', the lamb cried 'baa', and the spider skittered, 'scrickety-scrack', back into his web.

It was just an ordinary stable. With ordinary stable sounds…

And one extraordinary baby boy!

A Flock of Angels

That busy angel, Gabriel, had one more
Christmas job to do. He had to tell somebody
that the baby, Jesus, had been born.

He could have told a powerful somebody
– like the king.

He could have told a religious somebody –
like the high priest.

Or he could have told a wealthy somebody
– like the richest man in Bethlehem.

But instead he told the shepherds – plain and ordinary somebodies. Somebodies like you and me!

They were watching their sheep, out on a hillside. It was late. It was dark. And some of them just wanted to drop off to sleep.

And that's when Gabriel appeared – bright and shiny, glowing and gold – just as he had appeared to Mary and to Zechariah.

'Don't be afraid!' he said to the shepherds, and he smiled when he realized how silly that sounded.

Of course they were afraid! Who wouldn't be? They had never seen an angel before.

And so they were trembling and shaking, just like frightened sheep.

'I have good news for you!' Gabriel explained. 'God has sent someone very special, to bring joy to this dark world. And tonight that someone has been born – not far from here in Bethlehem! Go, and you will find him, a baby bundled up tight and lying in a manger.'

And then, suddenly, Gabriel was not
alone.

The angels that joined him looked like
sheep, at first, bright against the dark sky-
reflections of the beasts on the hill below. But
as the shepherds watched, the angels spread
their wings and began to sing:

'Glory to God in heaven,

And peace to men on earth!'

And when they had finished, they
disappeared, leaving the shepherds alone.

It took no time at all. The shepherds
leaped to their feet and went to Bethlehem.
There they found Mary and Joseph, and
the baby in the manger. And when they
described what they had seen – to the
innkeeper and his wife and anyone else who
would listen – everyone wondered and was

amazed. Everyone but Mary, that is, who
nodded and smiled as if she had expected
just this sort of thing to happen.

Then, singing and laughing, the
shepherds went back to the hills. But they
kept their eyes trained on the sky, just in case
another bright flock of angels should appear!

The Star That Went Zoom!

Twinkle – twinkle, went the stars. And the star-watchers nodded and smiled.

'There's a pretty one!' the first star-watcher said.

'And look how brightly that one is shining,' said the second star-watcher.

'And the big one – the big one over there,' cried the third star-watcher. 'I don't think I've ever seen one so huge!'

Twinkle-twinkle, went the stars. And then one of the stars went Zoom!

'Did you see that?' asked the first star-watcher.

'Couldn't miss it!' said the second.

'What do you suppose it means?' wondered the third.

So they all ran for their special star-watching books.

Twinkle-twinkle, went the stars. And the star-watchers read and searched and scratched their heads. 'It's not an earthquake,' said the first star-watcher. 'We can be grateful for that!'

'And it's not a flood, either,' said the second.

That's when the third star-watcher went 'Aha! I've found it! A zooming star means that, somewhere, a new king has been born!'

'But where?' asked the other star-watchers.

'There's no way to tell,' said the third star-watcher, 'unless we follow the star and see where it stops.'

'Then let's do it!' said the first star-watcher, putting on his hat.

'Sounds good to me,' said the second, as

he pulled on his long coat.

'I'll need to find someone to mind the cat,' said the third. 'But I'd like to go as well.'

And so the star-watchers gathered their servants and loaded their camels. And with the stars twinkle-twinkling above, they set off after that special star – the star that went Zoom!

The star zoomed left. The star zoomed right. Over hills it zoomed, and deserts and rivers and mountain peaks.

The star-watchers did their best to zoom after it. But the hills were high, and the deserts were hot. The rivers were deep, and the mountain peaks were hard to climb. And that was why it took them so long to follow the star.

For days and weeks and months they

travelled, until finally the star stopped, and
they found themselves in Judea, at the edge
of the Great Sea.

'This is the land of the Jews,' said the first
star-watcher.

'Then the baby must be their new king,'
said the second.

'So let's find the palace,' suggested the
third star-watcher, 'and give him the honour
he deserves.'

They thought they had it all worked out,
and so the star-watchers headed for

Jerusalem and the palace of the king. But what they failed to notice was that the star had zoomed somewhere else!

The star-watchers asked everyone they met.

'We have come from the East,' they explained. 'We are looking for a king. Perhaps you could help us find him – the newborn King of the Jews.'

Everyone was surprised by the question.

And no one more than King Herod.

'What do they mean?' he shouted at his advisers. 'I am the King of the Jews!'

'Y-Yes, of c-course,' stammered the frightened men. 'B-But perhaps they are looking for the special king – the one God promised us, many years ago.'

'And where would they find such a king?' Herod growled.

'In B-Bethlehem,' the advisers stammered again. 'At least, that's what the prophets say.'

'I see,' Herod muttered. And then his eyes began to twinkle-twinkle like two dark stars. 'Send for these star-watchers,' he commanded. 'I have something to ask them.'

The star-watchers came as quickly as they could. And once Herod had sent away his advisers, he leaned over to the star-watchers and whispered, 'The king you are looking for is in the town of Bethlehem. I want you to go there – it's not far – and when you

have found him, I want you to return and tell me exactly where he is – so that I might honour him too.'

The star – watchers nodded and bowed. They thanked the king and then headed straight for Bethlehem. But what they did not know was that Herod was an evil king – a king determined to kill anyone who tried to take his throne – even a little baby boy in Bethlehem!

Gifts for a King

When the star-watchers arrived in
Bethlehem, the star was already waiting for
them there. But it was no longer zooming.
Instead, it crept along slowly, leading them
through the narrow streets of the town. And
then, suddenly, it stopped, and hovered
silently over a very ordinary-looking house.

'This must be the place,' said the first star-
watcher.

'It doesn't look much like a palace,' said the second.

'Well, we shall have to go in and see for ourselves,' said the third. And he knocked, politely, on the door.

An ordinary-looking man opened the door – a man as ordinary as the house.

'We're very sorry,' said the first star-watcher. 'We must have the wrong place.'

'Forgive us for troubling you,' apologized the second.

'But the star…' whispered the third star-watcher to the others, 'The star is right overhead.' And then he turned to the man at the door. 'We're looking for a king – the newborn King of the Jews. I don't suppose you have a baby here?'

And with that, the ordinary-looking man smiled. A secret smile. A knowing smile.

For this man was Joseph.

'As a matter of fact, we do,' he said. 'Little Jesus is almost a year old, now, but I think he's the one you're looking for.'

The star-watchers filed into the house. The child was sitting on his mother's lap, playing with her fingers. And as soon as they saw him, they knew they were in the right place.

One by one, the star-watchers fell to
their knees before him. Then they gave him
presents – presents they had brought all the
way from the East. But they weren't the kind
of presents that most people give to babies.
No rattles or building blocks or soft toys.

No, they were presents fit for a king:

Bright, shiny gold.

A rich perfume called myrrh.

And frankincense, a sweet-smelling oil.

The baby patted the gold, and the jar that held the oil. But when he very nearly tipped over the bottle of perfume, his mother gently took his hand. 'Thank you,' she said to the star-watchers. 'It was kind of you to come.'

And so the star-watchers stood and bowed and said their goodbyes. It was too late to return to Jerusalem, so they set up their tents on the outskirts of town. But as they lay there asleep, each of the star-watchers had a dream. There was a visitor, bright and shiny, glowing and gold (that busy angel, Gabriel, perhaps?). And the visitor had a message.

'King Herod wants to kill the child,' the message warned them. 'You must not return to him. Go back to your homes, instead. Go quickly! And you will save the child's life.'

So the star-watchers rose at once. They folded their tents. They loaded their camels. And, rubbing the sleep from their eyes, they started for home, the stars twinkle-twinkling like gold to light their way.

King Herod's Evil Plan

King Herod frowned.

King Herod scowled.

King Herod clenched his teeth and scrunched up his face.

And then King Herod shouted. 'THE STAR-WATCHERS ARE GONE?!'

'Y-Yes, Your Majesty,' his advisers muttered. 'At least that is what we have heard.'

'But they were supposed to return to me! They were supposed to tell me where I could find this newborn king!'

'W-well, we know he's in Bethlehem,' said the advisers.

'Of course he's in Bethlehem!' the king shouted again. 'Along with hundreds of other babies…' And as soon as he'd said it, the king's face changed.

He no longer frowned.

He no longer scowled.

He no longer clenched his teeth or scrunched up his face.

No, King Herod began to smile – a dark and cruel smile.

'Leave me!' he commanded. 'And send in the captain of my guard.'

That smile was still on Herod's face when

the captain entered and bowed.

'I have a job for you,' the king explained.

'I want you to go to Bethlehem and kill…
oh, let us say, every male child two years old
and under.'

The captain did not smile.

He did not frown, either.

He just stood there with his lips pressed
tightly together.

His eyes showed his surprise, however, for this was the most awful thing he had ever heard.

'Well, get on with it!'the king commanded. 'You have your orders. And there are plenty of others,' he added, 'who would love to have your job.'

And so the captain left and rounded up his soldiers. And they set off to kill all of Bethlehem's baby boys.

Joseph slept. He had a sweet, sleepy smile on his face. But his smile turned to a worried frown when the visitor appeared to him in a dream. It was that busy angel, Gabriel, again. 'Get up, Joseph,' he said. 'Take the child and his mother and go to Egypt. Herod's soldiers are on the way. And they mean to kill the boy.'

Joseph got up at once. He nudged Mary awake and quietly they packed their things. Then she bundled up the sleeping Jesus and, together, they slipped off into the night.

They stayed in Egypt until King Herod died. Then they returned to Nazareth where Jesus grew up – the son of a carpenter and God's own special Son as well!

The Littlest Camel

christmas tales and legends

from around the world

Contents

The Little Lambs

Once upon a time, there were two little lambs. They lived with their flock on a hill outside Bethlehem. And every night, before they fell asleep, they would sit around the fire and listen to the tales of a wise, old shepherd.

Some of the stories were exciting, and the little lambs could hardly get to sleep.

Some tales were funny, and the little

lambs would roll with laughter.

Others were scary, and the little lambs would snuggle extra close to their mother sheep.

But one night, the old shepherd told a special tale – a story about something that was yet to happen.

'One day,' he said slowly, 'one day, a king

will be born. He will be powerful. He will be good. And he will put right what is wrong in this world. But here is the amazing thing!

He will not be born in a palace. He will not be born to the rich and the mighty. No – he will be born to poor and ordinary people. People just like us!'

The two little lambs had never heard such a thing.

'A king!' said the first.

'A king and a shepherd!' said the second.

And secretly, they both wondered the same thing: Where is this king? And when can we go and see him?

One crisp, clear night, a few weeks later, the old shepherd told the story again. And when he had finished, one lamb turned to the other.

'I want to see this king!' he whispered.

'Me too!' said the second little lamb.

'Why don't we try to find him – tonight!'

And so they pretended to go to sleep.

They shut their eyes. They baa-ed and they snuffled and they snored. And when their mother sheep was finally fast asleep, they sneaked out of the sheepfold and hurried down the hill.

They peeped into the shepherds' huts first. No baby there.

Then they crept around every dimming campfire. No king there, either.

'What now?' asked the first lamb.

The second lamb thought for a minute.

And then he said just one word: 'Grass.'

'Grass?' asked the first lamb.

'Yes,' nodded the second. 'When we are

looking for grass, we go from hill to hill, don't
we? And the shepherd never stops until he
finds the greenest pasture. That's what we'll
do. We'll never stop, until we find the king!'

And so they searched – from hill to hill
and valley to valley, halfway through that
dark night. But still they found no baby king.

At last, they came to a road.

'I'm tired,' said the first lamb. 'I want to
go home!'

'But here is a road!' said the second lamb. 'Maybe it will take us to the king!'

'You go if you want to,' the first lamb sighed. 'I'm going back.' And that's just what he did.

But the second little lamb would not give up. So he started down that road.

It was dark and it was late and he was frightened. So the little lamb tried hard to remember the old shepherd's funny stories. And he tried even harder to forget the scary ones!

Suddenly, the sky turned bright. Behind him, over the hills, there was light and – could it be? – singing! And ahead of him, the sky seemed brighter too. For a star shone high in the heavens, lighting up a little town below.

The little lamb started to run. Something special was happening, and he wanted to see it, even if it had nothing to do with that special king.

He followed the star to a stable. And there, among the sleepy beasts, were a mother and a father and a baby.

The lamb crept in and nuzzled the child. The child patted the lamb on his woolly head. And it wasn't long before the shepherds, and their sheep – and his tired brother too – came creeping in as well.

'What are you doing here?' asked the old shepherd, when he spotted the little lamb. 'I know. You're here to see the king I told you about.' Then he pointed at the baby. 'Well, there he is. A good king. A powerful king. A king who will, one day, put right what is wrong with this world. A king born poor and ordinary – just like us!'

The Raven

Raven was a jealous bird.

He was jealous of Robin and Bluebird and Dove, for they were more beautiful than him.

And he was jealous of Sparrow and Nightingale too, for he could never hope to sing like them.

So Raven flew through the night skies, a sad and bitter shadow, calling out his lonely caw-caw.

One cold December night, Raven sensed suddenly that he was not alone. He felt the sky above him shiver, as if he were in the wake of some much larger bird – Eagle, perhaps, or Vulture. But then Raven heard singing too – singing so lovely that it could never have come from the throats of those two high-flying hunters.

Jealousy struck Raven first. Why should he bother with yet another bird and its golden voice? But curiosity was there as well. And so, fighting his jealousy, Raven looked up into the sky. And there, floating above him, were no birds at all, but a flock of golden angels!

'Good news!' the angels sang. 'We have good news! God's own Son is born in Bethlehem tonight! And you, Raven, must

go and tell all the other birds!'

'Me?' Raven croaked. 'Why me? I am
the ugliest of the birds, and as for my voice –
well, you can hear for yourselves! They will
never listen to me.'

'But you have been chosen,' the angels sang. And, without another word, they flew off into the night.

What could Raven do? The birds had to know. And he, of all birds, had been chosen to tell them. And so he flew down from the sky, down to the tree tops – his cry as sharp and piercing as the winter night.

'Christ is born!' he called – called to Robin and to Bluebird and to Dove. 'Born in Bethlehem tonight!'

'Then we must go and see him,' they chirped. And Raven was surprised, for not one of them mentioned how ugly Raven was.

'Christ is born!' he called again – called to Sparrow and to Nightingale.

'Then we must go and sing to him!' they twittered. And again Raven was surprised,

for not one of them said a thing about the harshness of Raven's voice.

And so Raven flew to Bethlehem too.

He watched the baby reach out and touch Robin's red breast. He heard the baby giggle and coo along with Nightingale's sweet lullaby. And he wished that he could do something more than perch high in the stable's dark rafters.

'But don't you see?' came a voice –
a sweet sing-song voice amid the flutter of
golden wings. 'You have done the most
important thing of all. For none of the other
birds would be here, if you had not pierced
the night with your cries and told them the
good news.'

Then the angel disappeared. And leaving
his jealousy behind, Raven took flight too –
down from the rafters to join the others at
the side of the child.

The Littlest Camel

'Hurry along!' snorted the Big Brown Camel from the back of the caravan. 'Hurry along, or we'll never catch up!'

'He's going as fast as he can!' said Mother Camel. 'You can't ask for more than that.'

And the Littlest Camel? The Littlest Camel said nothing. For it was all he could do to keep his little legs moving.

Up the sand dunes and down the sand

dunes. Over the mountains and across the
rocky plains.

He had done nothing but walk for weeks.
And when the walking was over, he would
sleep – fast and deep – snuggled at his
mother's side.

'He shouldn't even be here!' grunted the
Big Brown Camel. And he spat on the dusty
track. 'He's not big enough to carry
anything. And he's slow. Much too slow!'

'But it's not his fault!' said Mother Camel.
'How many times do I have to tell you? The

camel driver made a mistake. He picked me
out at the market – just where he bought
you – but he didn't see my baby beside me.
And by the time we reached the desert and
he noticed, it was too late to turn back.'

'Well, I'm not going to get left behind.
I promise you that!' the Big Brown Camel
grunted.

Again, the Littlest Camel didn't say a
word. He just tried to keep his legs moving.
One, two, three, four. One, two, three, four.

And that's when somebody shouted, 'The

star has stopped! Look, there's the town.'

'It won't be long now, dear,' said Mother Camel. And the Littlest Camel smiled. He couldn't wait to rest his weary legs. But as they entered the town, everyone started to speed up, for the men at the front of the caravan were anxious to reach their destination.

Maybe that's why it happened. Or perhaps it was because the Big Brown Camel was in such a hurry. But when they turned a corner in one of Bethlehem's narrow streets, the Littlest Camel tripped and fell tumbling to the ground.

The Big Brown Camel stepped right over him. 'I'm not waiting for you!' he grunted.

And even though Mother Camel turned and tried to stop, the camel driver was in

such a rush that he whipped her back into
the line.

The Littlest Camel picked himself up, leg
by bony leg. Then he ran as fast as those
legs would carry him, after his mother and
the rest of the caravan. Through the streets
he followed them, always just that bit too far
behind.

But when they finally stopped – beasts
and men alike, falling on their knees before

a simple stable – the Littlest Camel could not slow down! And so he tripped and tumbled one more time –past camels and servants and three men with bright gifts – and landed head-first at the foot of a wooden manger.

The Littlest Camel shook his head.

The Littlest Camel opened his eyes.

The Littlest Camel was face-to-face with a little baby!

The baby smiled at him and patted his camel nose.

And that's when the camel heard these words: 'Well done, little camel. You travelled far to see my Son. And you never gave up. So from now on, it will be a camel, the Littlest Camel, who will bring gifts to the children of this land.'

And that is why, to this day, children in the Middle East receive their Christmas gifts from the back of a camel – a little camel, just like the one who brought joy to the child in the manger.

Old Befana

Shoop, shoop, shoop. Old Befana swept the floor.

Shoop, shoop, shoop. She swept out the cupboards too.

Shoop, shoop, shoop. Old Befana swept up every bit of dirt, every tumbling dustball and every little crumb.

Old Befana's house was spotless! And her front step too. And the path that led to the road.

Sweeping was all that Old Befana did. It was all that Old Befana loved. And so she was annoyed when, early one morning, in the midst of her sweeping, she was disturbed by a loud Bang, Bang, Bang! on the door.

She opened the door, the broom still in her hand. And she was greeted by three tall, tired strangers.

'We have travelled all night,' said the first stranger.

'We are following a star,' explained the second.

'And we need somewhere to sleep,' begged the third.

Old Befana looked at the three men. They were very well dressed. There were jewels on their hats and on their gowns and on the chains that hung round their necks. They

could have been rich merchants, or wizards,
or kings. In any case, they did not look like
robbers. And as for her sweeping – well, the
bedroom had already been swept for the
day. So she nodded her head and welcomed
them in.

She showed them the way to the bedroom,
and when she looked in on them a few
minutes later, she discovered that they were
all fast asleep in one bed – the covers pulled
up tight under their big beards!

Old Befana returned to her sweeping.

Shoop, shoop, shoop. She swept the kitchen.

Shoop, shoop, shoop. She swept the living room too.

Shoop, shoop, shoop. She swept the step and the path to the road.

And all the while she swept, she wondered, 'Where do they come from? Where are they going? And why do they sleep all day?'

So when, at last, the three strangers awoke, she asked them.

'We come from the East,' said the first stranger, 'and have travelled all night.'

'We are following a star,' said the second.

'A star that will lead us to the King of all Kings,' explained the third. 'A king who is but a little child!'

Then the three strangers made Old Befana a most unusual offer.

'Since you have been so kind to us…' began the first stranger.

'And since you have given us a place to rest…' continued the second.

'We would like you to come with us!' invited the third, 'to see this king and to bring him gifts!'

Old Befana was so surprised that she

nearly dropped her broom. What an
adventure! she thought. To follow a star
and find a king!

But then she looked at her broom. And
she looked around her house. And it didn't
take her long to imagine how dusty
everything would be if she ceased her

sweeping for even one day.

So she sadly shook her head and said, 'No, thank you.' And the three strangers walked off into the night.

Old Befana went to sleep, but her dreams were interrupted by visions of strangers and stars and kings. The next morning, she picked up her broom, as usual, but try as she might, she could not keep her mind on her sweeping.

Shoop, shoop, shoop. She swept the living room. But all she could think of was the strangers' invitation.

Shoop, shoop. She swept the kitchen. But all she could think of was that wandering star.

Shoop. She swept the front step. But all she could think of was the little king – who was down that road, somewhere, in a house, with a path and a step like hers.

And that's when she decided she would join the strangers after all. So with the broom in one hand, and an apron full of little gifts, she set off down the road.

She walked and she walked. She searched and she searched. But, sadly, Old Befana

never did find the three strangers. And, so they say, she is walking still – with a broom in her hand and with an apron full of gifts. And each Christmas, she walks up every path, climbs up every step and visits every house. And wherever she finds a child, she leaves a little gift. For she never can be certain which of those children is the 'King of all Kings'!

The Icicles

Through the woods they walked – Joseph
and Mary and little Jesus.

King Herod was dead. They were safe at
last. And so they were going home – all the
way from Egypt to Nazareth.

The days were warm enough. Too warm,
sometimes. So they would rest, when they
could, in some welcoming shadow.

But the nights were cold – especially the

nights in the hills. And this night was the coldest of them all!

The trees looked down on them and shook their leafless branches.

'They'll freeze to death!' said the cedar.

'They must find shelter,' said the birch.

'And look at the little boy,' sighed the pine tree. 'He can hardly keep from shivering.'

'But what can we do?' asked the cedar. 'My branches are bare. The wind will blow right through them.'

'Mine are no better,' nodded the birch.

And then they both looked at the pine tree.

'Of course!' she shouted. 'Why didn't I think of it myself?' And at once, she began to shake her furry boughs – so hard and so strong that Mary and Joseph could not fail to notice her.

'Look!' cried Joseph. 'A pine tree! If we huddle together beneath the branches, perhaps we can keep the wind out, and stay warm through the night.'

Mary agreed.

And little Jesus just shivered. So the three of them crept under the prickly pine boughs and wrapped themselves up in their blankets.

The wind blew and blew. The night grew frosty and sharp. Snowflakes began to fall. But through it all, Joseph and Mary and little Jesus slept safe and warm.

'They're still alive!' said the cedar to the pine tree.

'I think you've saved them!' added the birch.

And then the pine tree heard another voice – the glad song of a passing angel.

'Well done, pine tree!' the angel sang. 'For your warm boughs have sheltered the Son of God, himself!'

The pine tree could hardly believe it.

And in her excitement, she began to weep – tears of happiness, tears of joy! The tears trickled down her bushy branches. And as they trickled, they froze – froze in long, icy strands, all the way down to the ground.

When Mary and Joseph and Jesus awoke the next morning, they crawled out from under the tree. And what they saw made the little boy jump with delight.

'Look!' he called. 'Look at all the pretty icicles.'

And so they were, shining like diamonds in the morning sun.

And perhaps that is why some people still dress their Christmas trees with icicle decoration – in memory of that clever pine tree and her beautiful frozen tears.

The First Christmas Tree

Boniface was walking through the woods.
It was winter. It was cold. But even though
Boniface was desperate for a hot drink and
a warm fire, he kept on walking. For it was
his job to travel, from one end of England
to the other, telling the people about Jesus.
Boniface heard a cry. It was a child's cry.
A frightened cry. So Boniface stopped
walking and began to run.

The branches snapped at his face. The wind howled about him. But he was getting closer, he could tell, for the child's cries were growing louder.

At last, Boniface stumbled into a clearing. There, gathered at the foot of an oak tree, was a group of men – and the child's cry came from the midst of them.

'Stop!' Boniface shouted. 'Stop what you are doing! Now!'

The men turned towards him. Their faces were painted with strange and frightening patterns and each one held a weapon.

'Go away!' one of them called back. 'This is no business of yours!'

'Yes it is!' Boniface replied. 'For I can tell, by your dress and by your face-paint, that you are Druids. And if I am not mistaken, you intend to kill that boy and offer him as a sacrifice to one of your tree gods.'

'The god of the oak demands it!' one Druid argued. 'And we are here to serve him.'

'Well, I serve another God!' argued Boniface. 'A God who does not approve of the killing of children.' And with that, he grabbed an axe and began to chop at the

base of the oak tree. One of the Druids went to stop him, but the leader held him back.

'Wait,' he said with a sneer. 'The god of the oak tree will punish him soon enough!'

Boniface chopped and chopped. He chopped until he had chopped that oak tree down. And as it crashed to the forest floor, the Druids began to tremble.

'I don't understand,' said their leader.

'The god in the oak tree did nothing to protect himself – and nothing to punish you!'

'That's because there is no god in the tree!' Boniface explained. 'There is only one God – the God who made the tree, and everything else in this world. The God who does not demand the sacrifice of our sons. No, for he has already sacrificed his own Son, Jesus – sacrificed him on a tree – to take away all that is wrong in this world.'

'He sacrificed his own son?' said the Druid leader in wonder.

'Yes,' said Boniface. 'And more amazing than that, he brought his Son back to life again, so that we could live for ever too!'

And then Boniface pointed to a tree. Not the fallen oak, but a bright, furry evergreen.

'If you want to remember the God I

serve,' Boniface said, 'you could use that tree – the tree that never dies. Decorate it, and use it to celebrate the birth of Jesus – the Son of God, who lives for ever!'

So that's what the Druids did. And some people say that was the very first Christmas tree!

Francis' Christmas Pageant

The village of Greccio sat on a wooded hill across the valley from Mount Terminillo. On the rocky slopes of that mountain there were caves. And in one of those caves a man named Francis had built a little church.

Francis was a good man, a saint. He rebuilt broken-down churches, helped broken-down people, and travelled across this poor broken-down world talking about the love of God.

One cold Christmas Eve, Francis decided to do something special for the people who lived in Greccio. He called together his friends, a group of monks called the Little Brothers, and he asked them to bring him a wooden manger. He asked for a donkey as well. And a big brown cow. And when he had put them in the cave, he sent out the Little Brothers again.

'Go to the village,' he said. Invite everyone. Tell them there is something special waiting for them in the cave.'

The monks did as they were asked and it wasn't long before Francis could see the villagers streaming up the mountainside: A boy with a stick, a little girl, a baker and blacksmith and a fat old man. A jester and a soldier. A tall man on a horse with a fine lady beside him. A crippled old woman and a beggar and a priest.

They were all there, every one, carrying torches to light their way, so bright against the dark hillside that they could have been stars on that first Christmas night, or the angels who sang to the shepherds.

When they reached the cave, Francis called one woman forward to kneel, like Mary, at the manger's side. Then he asked a man to stand and watch over her, like Joseph. Finally, Francis began to sing. He sang the story of that first Christmas, and the

people of Greccio wept when they heard
how God had chosen a poor woman, poorer
even than themselves to give birth to his own
Son, Jesus.

And so they sang God's praises through
the night – Saint Francis and the people of
Greccio, at the very first Christmas pageant!

The First Tinsel

It was Christmas Eve and, at last, everything was quiet.

The children had finally forced themselves to sleep.

Mother and Father were snoring away, exhausted, in their bed.

And even the mice were snuggled safe in their holes.

So that's when the spiders came out –

crawling through the crack in the corner of the ceiling.

'The coast is clear!' called Mr Spider.

'I'm coming as fast as I can!' called his wife in return.

It was the same every night. They would anchor two long, sticky strands to the ceiling, and swing across the room, down to the floor on the other side. Then they would snip the silky strands and explore! Up and down the curtains they would go, over and under each chair. And if, along the way, they happened to stumble across a wandering fly or a wayward ant, then they would enjoy a midnight snack as well!

'Hang on tight!' said Mr Spider.

'Eight legs' worth!' said Mrs Spider in return.

And with a leap and a 'Yahoo!' the

spiders sailed across the room.

They should have reached the far end of the room, just as normal. But it was Christmas Eve, remember? So instead of landing on the floor, they crashed into something tall and prickly!

'It's a tree!' called Mr Spider. 'I'm pretty sure it's a tree!'

'But it wasn't here last night,' wondered Mrs Spider. 'How did it grow so fast?'

'Perhaps we should explore it,' suggested Mr Spider.

'Excellent!' Mrs Spider agreed. And then, licking her lips, she added, 'I hear that grubs live in trees, and I haven't eaten a grub in a long time!'

So the spiders crawled down the tree. They started from the star at the top.

Mr Spider went one way.
Mrs Spider went the other.
And they were both so excited
that they forgot about snipping
off the long strands of web that
trailed behind them.

'Look, here's an orange!'
called Mr Spider.

'And an apple!' replied his
wife.

There were pine cones and
candles and bows and bells as
well – it was a tree full of
surprises! But suddenly, just as
they reached the bottom, the
lights in the room flickered
on. So Mr and Mrs Spider did
what any sensible spiders would

– they skittered far under the tree and into the darkest shadow they could find.

At first, they could see only boots. Big black boots with white fur around the tops. Then there were hands. White-gloved hands thrusting huge bright boxes right in front of their spider faces. Then there was chuckling – and the odd, deep 'Ho-ho-ho!' And finally, from that same deep voice, there boomed a 'What's this?'

The man with the black boots and the white gloves stood back and looked at the tree. And then he laughed again – another 'Ho-ho-ho!'

'A spider's been here,' he chuckled. 'And left its web all up and down and around this tree. It's a lovely decoration. It just needs… yes, that's it.'

And he touched the web with the tip of his white-gloved hand.

All at once, the web turned to silver, from the point where he touched it and all around the tree!

When the man had gone and it was dark again, the spiders crawled out from their hiding place. They looked up at the tree,

and at their web, now glistening like silver.

'It's beautiful!' said Mr Spider.

'A wonder!' said Mrs Spider in return.

And some say that's how the very first tinsel came to be!

A Flower for Christmas

Everyone was walking to the church.
Everyone in the little Mexican town. Their
arms were heavy with gifts – fruit and
vegetables and sweets – for it was Christmas
Eve and everyone was expected to bring a
present for the Christ Child.

Manuel watched them all walk by. He
watched them laugh. He watched them
sing. He watched the way they shared their

excitement and joy.

But all he could do was to wipe the tears from his dirty face, for Manuel was a child of the streets – a poor orphan boy with nothing at all to bring.

He had tried begging for something, but the people had only laughed. 'You say you want it for the Christ Child?' they sneered. 'We know your kind. You'll just keep it for yourself!'

He had thought about stealing something too. But stealing? For the Christ Child? Surely that would be worse than bringing no gift at all.

And so he kept his distance. And when the crowd had shuffled into the church, and when the doors had been shut behind them, he crept to an open window and peered in.

Everything was so beautiful – the candles, the decorations and the gifts! There were hundreds of them, piled up round the statue of the Christ Child and his mother.

But the longer Manuel looked, the sadder he felt, until finally, he fell to his knees and he prayed, 'Dear Christ Child, I am not like the people in the church. I have nothing to bring to you this Christmas Eve. So please accept my prayer. And my tears as well.

For they are all I have to give you.'

Manuel wiped his face dry again. Then he opened his eyes. And there, where his tears had fallen, was a flower. A flower that had not been there before. Gold as the star that shone over Bethlehem, that's how bright the flower was. And surrounding it, there were leaves as red as blood!

'It's a miracle!' Manuel cried. And he scooped up the flower, roots and all, and ran into the church.

'Look!' he shouted, running down the aisle. 'Look! I have a gift for the Christ Child too!'

Some people whispered and moaned.

They did not like their service interrupted. But when they saw the flower, their groans turned to sighs of wonder.

'It is a miracle, indeed!' the priest agreed. 'A flower such as I have never seen!'

And so it was that Manuel's poinsettia became known by the special name of 'The Flower of the Holy Night'!

A Note from the Author

As you may wish to read other versions of some of these traditional stories, I would like to acknowledge some of the sources I have referred to, although most of these stories can be found in several collections. You will find the stories listed under the titles used in this book, but they should be easy to identify in the books I mention.

'The Littlest Camel', 'The First Tinsel' and 'The Raven' from *Hark! A Christmas Sampler* by Jane Yolen, G.P. Putnam's Sons, New York, 1991. 'Old Befana', 'The First Christmas Tree', 'The Icicles', 'St Francis' Christmas Pageant' and 'A Flower for Christmas' from *It's Time for Christmas* by Elizabeth Hough Sechrist and Janette Woolsey, Macrae Smith Company, Philadelphia, 1959. 'The Little Lambs' from *Joy to the World* by Ruth Sawyer, Little, Brown and Company, Boston, 1966.

Also by Bob Hartman:

Collections

The Lion Storyteller Bible

The Lion Storyteller Bedtime Book

The Lion Storyteller Christmas Book

The Lion Storyteller Book of Animal Tales

Picture books

Dinner in the Lions' Den

Noah's Big Boat

The Three Billy Goats' Stuff!

The Wolf Who Cried Boy

All Lion books are available from your local bookshop, or can be ordered via our website or from Marston Book Services. For a free catalogue, showing the complete list of titles available, please contact:

Customer Services
Marston Book Services
PO Box 269
Abingdon
Oxon
OX14 4YN

Tel: +44 (0) 1235 465500
Fax: +44 (0) 1235 465555

Our website can be found at:
www.lionhudson.com